Rippling Waters of Solitude

Ameya Bondre

Rippling waters of Solitude

Ameya Bondre

First Published in July 2022

ISBN: 978-93-5628-389-3

www.BlueRoseONE.com
info@bluerosepublishers.com
+91 8882 898 898

Cover and Book design by Sagar Bhat

Distributed by: BlueRose, Amazon, Flipkart

For -
the mind,
the churning,
the mental
'lockdown'

Acknowledgements

I must thank the editorial team of my
medical college magazine in Mumbai
in 2005; a homeless man on the streets
of Mount Vernon in Baltimore in 2010,
who met a girl – she got down from a bus,
passed him, strolled casually, went several
steps ahead and returned… to drop a packet
of half-eaten sandwich that she had,
on his lap, and to tell him, 'please have it';
the creative writing workshop I was lucky
to enroll in, purely triggered by a random,
sudden thought of joining a fiction-writing
class in 2017; and the several instances of
crumpled paper, erased Word documents,
cancelled ideas and plot-lines, and the
now dissolved evenings in cafés, where I
soaked stories from around, and thought
through them.

I thank those situations, those days and
those people – I thank *them* all, as they
have been the reasons to write, to try to
write, to continue to write, and to put this
second book together.

I want to thank my parents for letting me
show them, this side of me, seeing
through it, and perhaps feeling surprised
and serenaded.

I want to thank my small, naïve, subjective, unformed, and deeply imperfect idea of a 'God', who is able to listen to silences more accurately than he listens to my incessant wish-making.

And, I must thank this gentleman, my friend called Joydeep Ghosh, who propelled the idea to draft or collate, rethink or redo, edit and express several of my 'poems' over an otherwise monotonous December of 2020.

Finally, how can I forget the sheer brilliance of the designer who made the cover and the interiors of this book? Sagar Bhat, this, is your artwork.

Table of Contents

Introduction

They never become waves. They never
make noise. They form, play around and
die. They form again. They spread, circle,
break and scatter. They never become waves
- waves that surge high, jump, and run to
the shore.

Such are the ripples – the thoughts,
musings and words in this book.

Are they *poems*? Probably. At least, some
of them. But they cannot be boxed into a
type. They try to connect the dots of rhyme,
rhythm, meter and structure. At times they
make it, at times they fail. They cannot be
boxed. They are the results of situations
and moods, solitude and crowds, faces and
memories, noise, and expressionless silence.
They are fickle and fleeting as the ripples,
steady and rooted as the water that holds
them. They point to no one. They follow no
rules. They have got titles, but they cannot
be named. They need each other though,
to stand by each other, to stay and stick on
these pages. They need shelter.

*"Not knowing when the dawn will come
I open every door."*

\- Emily Dickinson

Calm

I am not calm, am I...
I fake silence, and brood inside.
I race towards the sand
and, pull myself back.
I keep doing that.
I don't know whom to touch.
I rush, I wander for more.
An empty blue ocean that I am,
I wait for the Moon,
till ripples become tides.
I set them free, till they return,
trap me in a cycle I never wanted.
I horde them, who rattle me.
I look at a Moon, who smiles back,
I wait for him,
who's too far away.
I am the lost giant.
I have lost boundaries.
I am the deadpan.
I am the vastness.
I am imprisoned.
I am not calm, not me.

Searching

I fixed my gaze,
losing the sense of my stiffness
I stared at the centre of a table,
at the tray of glasses, placed upside down.
Those unmoving quiet glasses.
I tried to shut off the voices,

I tried to shut off the voices,
the chitter chatter of wives, husbands, partners,
girlfriends, fiances, sons and daughters,
They had taken a tea break,
sitting across a barren round table, a group of
romance artists in the middle of a lecture,
sharing personal lives and routines.

A married man pulled out his phone and showed
pictures of his teenage children to his peer.
How elaborately he spoke of their eating habits!
His peer said why he and his wife didn't want
to have a child,
but a daily video-call with their poodle
was mandated, when he was away.

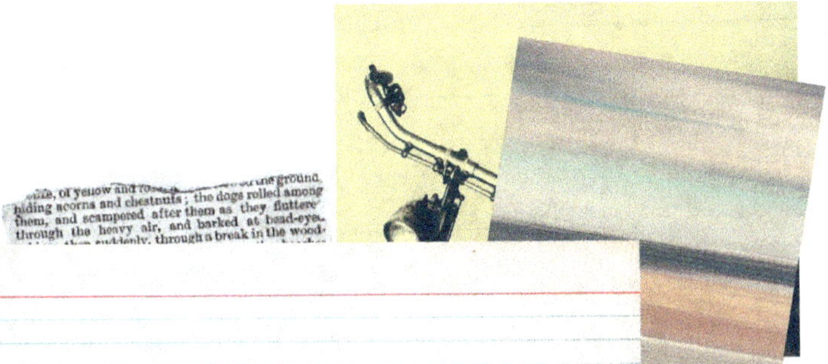

Another one spoke of his first date,'
when the tunes of a violin,
met their secretive glances,
over a candle light,

a candle that led,
such little conversation,
and such silly smiling.

And, I, kept, staring,
at the tray of glasses.
As if, searching
the ray of light
that passed through them,
but never met my eye,
Trying to shut off
the sounds of love
and its practising lovers.

Whirring

I am that one
who thinks he's Calm
the one staring at glasses...
I know what it wants,
the whirring in my head
it never settles on one
it never goes to bed.

I see crackers burst
Loud and sudden,
They try to twitch a face,
rigid, numb and sullen
I stare at Lights, from a table,
In an empty café
Lights, that rise and fly
and dissolve,
on this festive day.

I see families and groups
Huddled under lighted trees
I have my table, unlike these,
flat and bare,
resting at ease...

Whom do I meet this way
when my people are far away,
A home with a closed door
isn't a thing of today.

The whirring in my head,
needs a touch.
The roving eyes,
need a face.
The bottling of thoughts,
needs a smile
And the passing time,
feels like a race.

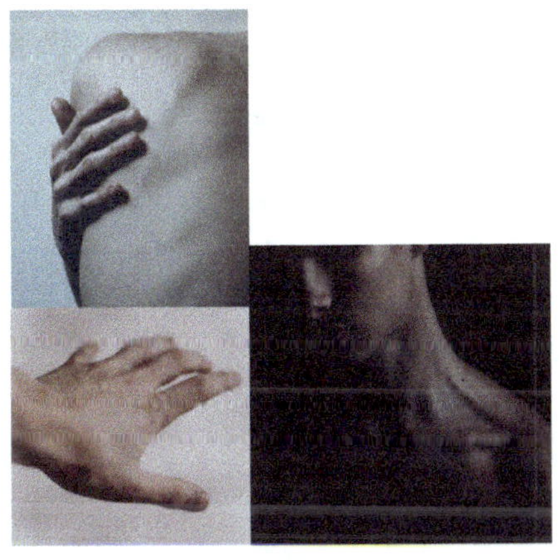

I want to break it
this form, this space
Reach out to someone
who's out of place!
Someone not festive
Someone inappropriate
Someone outcasted
You ask why?

I say, that's my lighted sky
A touch is what I'll get
A memory is what I'll forget
For the time I'll be with her
For the lights we'll oil and blur

It will be wrong,
untimely,
odd,
It will break rules, set on these
days!
It will feed the whirring,
in my head
That never settles for one.
That never goes to bed.

It will be a night of lamps
and lanterns,
watching us
trade love,
It will be Hidden
and closed
Needful
and imposed.

I'll return from it, calm
Letting her go...
I'll think of it
again,
Letting it glow.
I'll sit at a table
who's never a foe.

I'll stare at empty glasses
across minutes unbroken...
I'll see families going
to their places chosen...
I'll look back at my time
with a face frozen...
I'll sense a smile,
wanting to tear open.

Mist

I let a thought, fly away
Like an eyelash from a fist
Under closed eyes, a wish,
Lost its way
Like fingers on glass,
rubbing the Mist.

*"We often confuse what we wish for
with what is."*

- Neil Gaiman

Those Days

Those days, posed for a photo.
Those beaches stood in memory.
Those meetings hid in albums.
Those benches froze in history.
We met... along those days,
We held hopes in fickle ways,
We spoke in pleasing tones,
We shared a time, unknown.

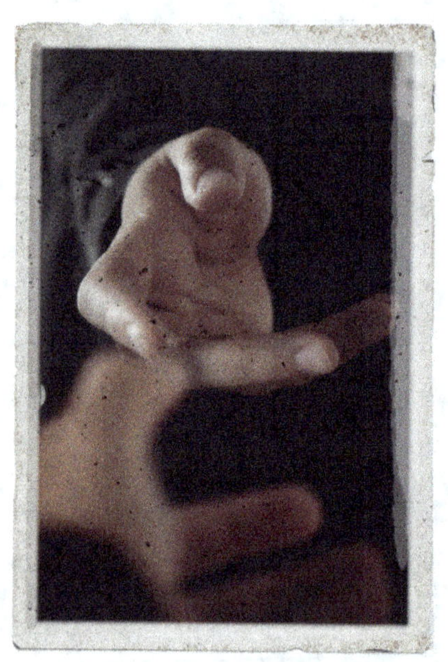

We didn't think enough,
We didn't want to feel rough,
We knew those were the days.
Days that watched our show.
That didn't let us know,
that our evenings set with the sun,
that our beaches came undone,
with flying sands of time,
with whispers worth a dime!
that we smiled for hope,
that we glided on a slope,
that we met, to part ways,
That we met... on posing days.

Home

I was running bare feet,
as we did in those little days,
on an empty street,
next to a railway track,
in black shorts,
and a creased white T-shirt,
with my friend,
always ahead of me.
It was the time of the day,
when the sun was at its peak,
the birds had slept,
the leaves didn't move,
on the few coconut trees
that watched over us,
and only the blaring engine
of a passing train,
could stop our sprint.
I saw a red Maruti 800,
racing towards me, and...
I fell on my face.
He stopped a few meters ahead.
My nose bled.
He rushed towards me,
pinched it hard,
and asked me to look up.
My hands and legs got stiff.
I got pale.
I said I cannot.

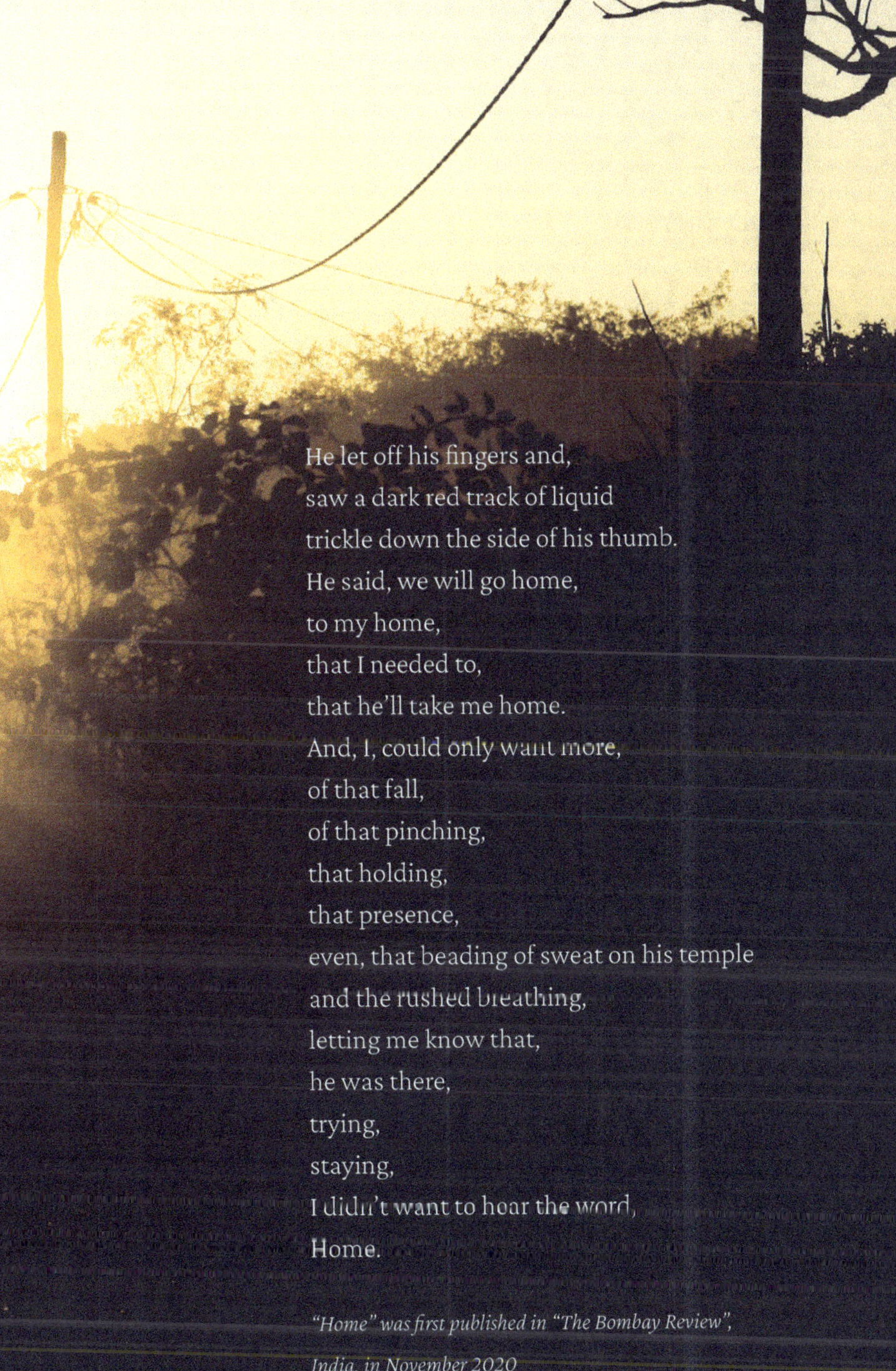

He let off his fingers and,
saw a dark red track of liquid
trickle down the side of his thumb.
He said, we will go home,
to my home,
that I needed to,
that he'll take me home.
And, I, could only want more,
of that fall,
of that pinching,
that holding,
that presence,
even, that beading of sweat on his temple
and the rushed breathing,
letting me know that,
he was there,
trying,
staying,
I didn't want to hear the word,
Home.

"Home" was first published in "The Bombay Review",

India, in November 2020

Ticking

And, I see hands
meet at midnight,
that wrap tight.
I watch them,
from a distance.
I move over.
I don't meet them.
I keep,
Ticking.

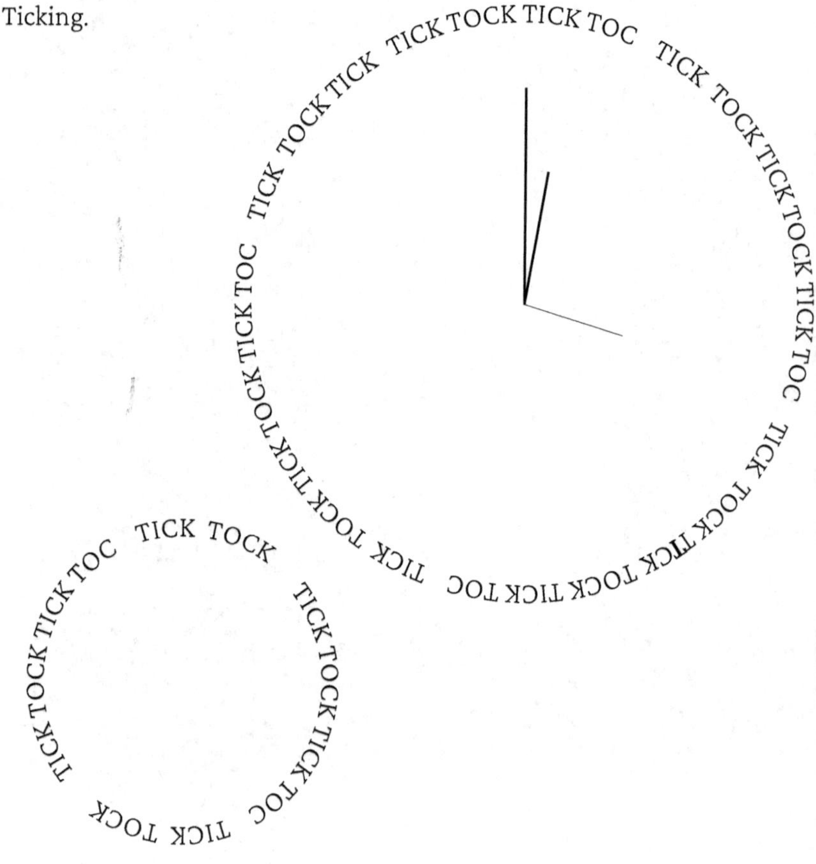

*"Think of many things. Never place
your happiness in one person's power.
Be just to yourself."*

- Vikram Seth

before I sleep...

Also,   I think,   before I sleep

A house of cards,

A gust of wind,

A fist of sand,

A castle so glorious...

To hold and keep.

An Ashtray

Even that name is constructed, not created.
It is not a finely moulded piece of glass.
It is not a proud owner of the particles strewn on it,
the grey and black dusted floor it shows.
An ashtray is an explanation.
A piece of comfort.
Something you would rest yourself on.
It's not without that sign... that finesse...
that manner, in which a burning cigarette is
brought closer to it. Barely touching its floor,
and yet dumped on it.

An **ashtray**, is an act of building elegant glassy walls,
to surround a slow, brewing crisis.
A habit, carefully protected, and supported,
over days and months and years of sparking,
lighting and burning, breathing and smelling.
Look at the transparency of its body,
allowing the sunlight to scatter.
Look at the calmness it embodies.
Look at its stability, its robustness.
Look at its warm, amiable, inviting, embrace.
Look at its Loyalty.
But where's the fourth wall?
Where are the limits?
Where's the ceiling?
Why does it have an open rooftop?

Is it like quicksand -
where one goes in, unaware, unrealized,
and slowly sinks in,
knowing fully what's happening under
the open sky?

"An Ashtray" was first published in the "Letters to Strangers", India in January 2021

Friendship

Friendship is,
too heavy a word.
It's hard to keep up with it,
over long distances,
longer time zones,
and mechanical routines.
And then, there are some friends...
like those short-lived co-travelers,
who meet you when you least expect.

You make eccentric memories,
cook fancy dinners,
laugh at lame jokes,
and end up having bitter-sweet arguments.

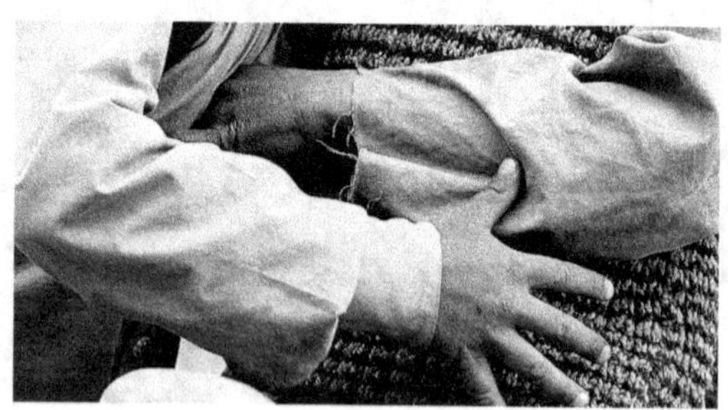

Whatever be the brutal impact of distance
and the passing months and years,
you think of them, and don't let them go.
You can still hold a fist of leaking sand,
and at the end,
see some of it stick on your palm,
staring at your face!

Conversation

It took a whole evening to smile.
It took a long sunset, to tide over.
The chill in the air broke a few hopes.
The rest, were unspoken.

A dark, blue place lit up by
yellow lights, crossing streets,
rushing people, and Christmas cheer.
They all waited for,
a conversation.

"In the best conversations, you don't even remember what you talked about, only how it felt. It felt like we were in some place your body can't visit, some place with no ceiling and no walls and no floor and no instruments."

\- John Green

Drift

I drift away
on a narrow lane,
Looking up and keen
with a sky so plain,
My thoughts on the cobblestone -
the feet... wax and wane,
I have windows to open,
And sunshine to gain.

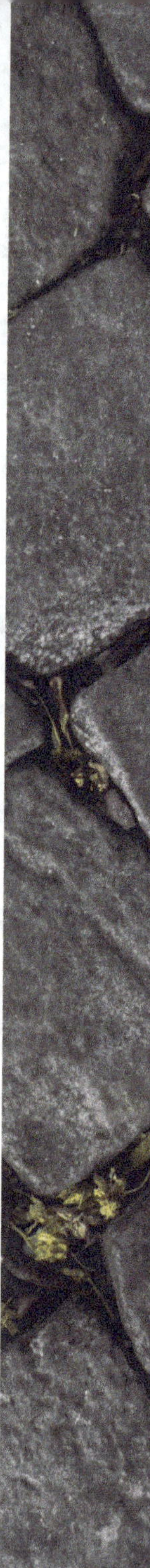

A Darling

She... was a darling. A minimalist lover. For a waiting-since-years-to-be-doggo daddy like me, she came with rays of sunshine in the biting Boston winter. Not so much into cuddles and tickles, she would just move around the couch, change her pace often, and almost mark a circle... where I, was allowed, wanted, and far from a stranger. Suddenly she would sit, all tired, curl a bit, and cling to my leg. Just that fleeting bit of contact. I would say silly somethings to her, and she would give a puzzled stare.

And, when it was time for me to leave, she would smell it, and run off to the bedroom. No parting hugs. No smiling Byes. No See You tail wags. She didn't want any of it. Going far far away from her... was simply unacceptable. She could brim her eyes with love, and let them do the talking. Hugs weren't her cup of tea.

She was,

a darling.

A Letter

Dear ex-friend,

We don't talk anymore. We seek help, for official work,
so the team can't see our tension. But we don't talk.
We don't make eye contact. When we cross each other,
we look down. It's cold, calculated, and cumbersome.
We plan our lunch time, in such a way that we
don't share the table. Even that sufficiently wide table.
But you like my posts on Instagram, and I do the same.
That's fine. Your like, on my post, is a reflex.
That like has no meaning. It's a click of a button.
A mechanical, rapid, heartless click, like the remains
of our equation...

There are no more questions or answers.
Let's not owe those to each other. We are too proud for that.
But, let's not stop mutually liking, our posts.
Let's do that bit of mechanics. The to and fro responses.
Behind our phones. Hiding behind machines.
Perhaps, if we keep doing that, we will keep getting,
a hint, that some part of us, is staying alive.
Some part of us, keeps a connection.

Regards
~~Ameya~~ Your ex-friend

The Reply

Dear Ameya,

I won't call you an ex-friend. Because, you have a name.
But you can be harsh with name-calling me. That's fine.
That's you. It's your reflex.
Yes, we shouldn't talk till we want to.

Both of us, thankfully, hate fakeness.
So, I won't stand your fake concern and you would find my fake
greetings, amusing. You would even call them 'amusing' on my face.
So, the silence is way better, and dignified.

Yes, the Instagram likes can continue. I will like your posts and
you may like mine.

We are hidden behind glittering screens.
No one is really watching us do that, while the world sees it.

And, what we do, under our own watch,
is slowly becoming inconsequential.

Yeah?

Regards,
Your ex-friend

Walls

Bare unsung walls, hide a forgotten time

Only for lone wanderers to find,

Bereft of meaning, robbed of their shine,

They get eyeballs and lenses to bind....

Paris

Paris lost to its people.
Crowds of tourists damaged her,
over the years, spilling litter.

The locals did feel xenophobic,
no dialogue, no persistent effort,
to engage a growing influx.

Anyway, some groups grabbed chances,
Radicals, Mentors in locked houses.
They waited for a reason.
They stayed in all seasons.

They picked up Charlie Hebdo.
They fueled anger on streets,
trapped politicians in vote banks.

JE SUIS CHARLIE

They rioted, looted and burned.
They revenged an arrogant city.
For years, as they saw.

QUARE
TRAL
ONS OF
STICE
HOSEN
THE
SO

Paris can only look inward,
what it was, and now,
what it has, and how.

Before it loses, all alone.
Before it loses its people.

"Paris" is a poem of limitations – each line is made up of five words.

Forget

If I could catch a drop, falling
or a leaf, flying
If I could throw a snowflake,
or kick a pebble
If you could stop, meeting me
as a flash in my head
Then, I may do better.
Forgive. Forget

"I could easily forgive his pride, if he had not mortified mine."

\- Jane Austen

Charm

They close your lids
not knowing what you hide,
A wide curious sky,
A yellow beam untied.

They cage you in charms –
Charms not letting you stray,
A world of song and colour
awaits you, far away.

No! The evil will touch you!
is what they say,
You are sacred, you are fragile,
We will show your way.

You carry weight, you cut grain,
You make pots, or you perform...
The charms won't let you 'sin'.
They can ward off a storm.

Who are they trying to hide?
Your colour, your glow, your hope?
Evil lies in the eyes that pry,
using tradition as a trope.

Behind hidden doors and dark curtains,
they all will ravage you,
slyly siding the divine charms,
meant to protect you.

I know you will wear them —
squares that fence your spirit,
Home, is an uneasy playground,
with a loving parent's writ.

Who is safe putting these on?
Who would come to your rescue?
Yes, you look up at the dark
the glimmer of stars mirror You!

Hope is a flickering flame
You have to let it burn
Time inches by your side
Tides take ages to turn.

You wear them!
You ignore them!
Your eyes, a wide curious sky
You'll shine as an image,
in an artist's mind.
You'll reach us, with a loud cry.

Our dreams and fears entwined,
Someone would come to you,
Our lives distant, far apart,
Someone would think about you.

Change is a hard nut,
You don't think about that,
Someone will hold your hand,
keeping the charms intact.

I will see you as an image,
again and again, in another time,
A story will change its track,
We will have mountains to climb!

Would you look different then?
Would you smile at me?
Would you own the charms?
Or would you set them free?

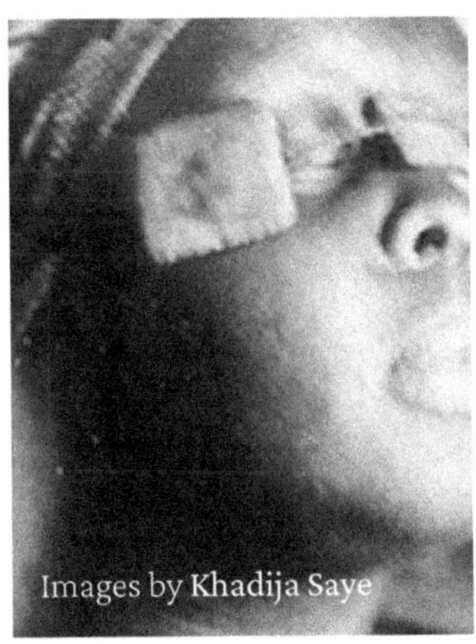

Khadija Saye, also known as **Ya-Haddy Sisi Saye**, was a Gambian-British artist, activist and carer. In both her life and work, Khadija was socio-politically engaged, and she dedicated herself to issues of social justice and educational inequality.

"Charm" was first published in the 'Visual Verse',
Vol-7, Chapter-9.

Please don't hold back...

a twinkle in your eye...
or one of your hidden tears...
why don't you tell me
each one of your fears...

who can say for sure,
when would we meet
again... or if we would?
please don't hold back,
it would do no good.

Felt your hand nervous... as it held mine
you want to say something...
don't you see?
just a hug, or some more time
means a lot now, Trust me.

you don't know how tough it is
to love... only to give someone away
you do know how easy it is
to let your silence... have all the say.

don't arrest... those arresting eyes!
and look at me in the eye
when time harshly flies,
don't let this moment die.

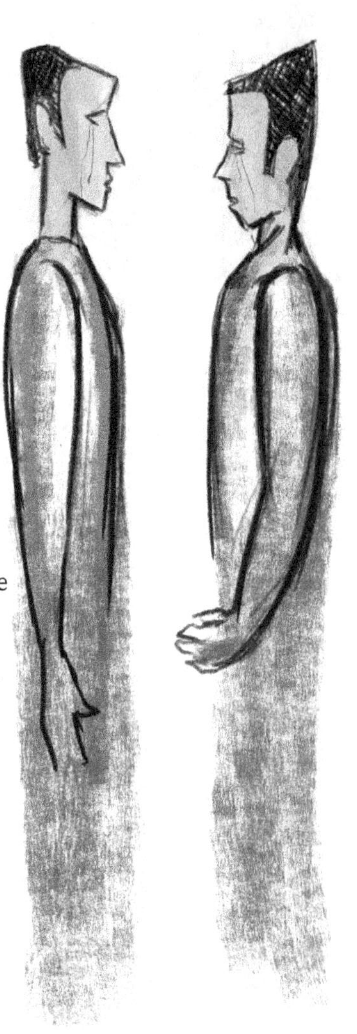

I am too weak now... to read between your lines
but too strong... to take your worries,
please, for the sake of our spent times...
let me break through lulls... as these.

feels great for what you chose...
to embrace new beginnings
but for once... say you want to...
would hold you so close,
set you free from your bindings.

some people aren't missed
even when they part their way
do they become a part of you
only to go away...?

You think holding back makes you tough...
or are you being tough on yourself?
just today, just for now, just for me,
don't hold back
when you shouldn't be.

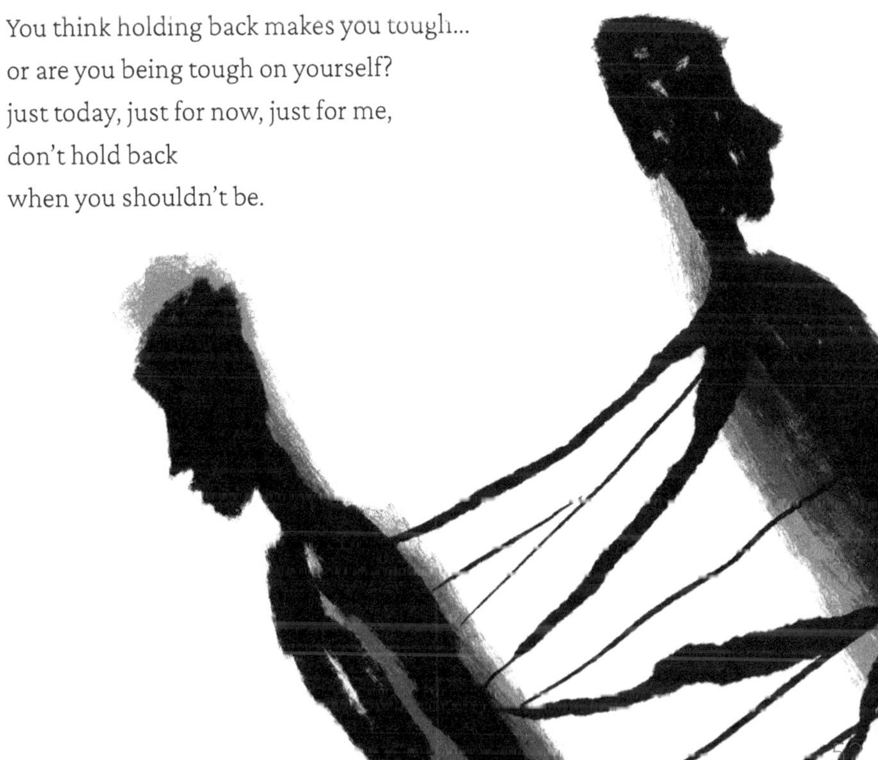

Weird

You are weird...

Yes!

Of course you are!

But you, can say -

You say things.

You, just say it!

As it is...

*"A sigh isn't just a sigh. We inhale
the world and breathe out meaning.
While we can."*

- Salman Rushdie

Try

A few piles of snow
On a sky so high
A home by the side
Sees a river flow shy
Give me a dog
And a mood to fly
I will walk over my bridges
And never stop to try.

"And now, Harry, let us step out into the night and pursue that flighty temptress, adventure."

- J.K. Rowling

Wind Chime

Stillness,
sounds of crickets,
bugs at the window,
muffling...
no voices,
no children outside,
dead air,
still curtains,
his own breaths,
he woke up
to deafening silenc
for days and days...
lazy eyes
gazed at..
the dark,
at the window,
a familiar sight...
he paused to see
the wind chime,
hung up in
soundless air,
he loved when it played
but today it didn't want to,
he smiled
for minutes and more,
staring at it.

he knew it would play,
the naughty one,
and loved his mind castles,
till,
A sudden breeze
gushing across
as if, all for him...
just poured in life,
the chimes rung
one by one,
they joined hands,
nudging each other to play,
And all together,
the notes jostled through them,
to breathe out,
spread across,
axed the stillness of the room,
touching his hands,
and taking them along,
he wanted to walk towards it,
being called to dance,
to come along
to get lost... for some time
to remind him
of... some time,
to caress the chimes,

to tell them that,
he missed something
so bad... so true... so much.
But the breeze had to stop.
so did the chimes,
the song,
the sync,
the notes,
the touch,
and the dance.
like a brilliant aurora, that had to fall
like the waves splashing at your feet
but soon slithering away...
like a meteor that dies...
He couldn't take any more
of the sickening silence
a deep breath...
some thoughts...
Madness...
He felt a surge within,
a certain energy,
he was being played along,
or made a joke...
He reached for those sound boxes
those beads,
those chimes,
the face they made,
their smiles,
the caricature,
Cruelty.
He pulled them hard,

With both his hands,
Pulled even more,
till the strings gave in...
He ravaged through,
till the chimes came off,
fell down on his feet,
died.
He pulled even more,
didn't want to leave any trace
wanted to kill it,
and all that it had,
But he gave in...
lost their sight,
his suppressed shriek
just made it... fall apart
Was it all over?
or just one of those things..
He gave a sigh.
a smile...
the silence
the same...
the dead air,
the curtains,
the breaths,
he owned it all,
he slept through,
And... through another night...

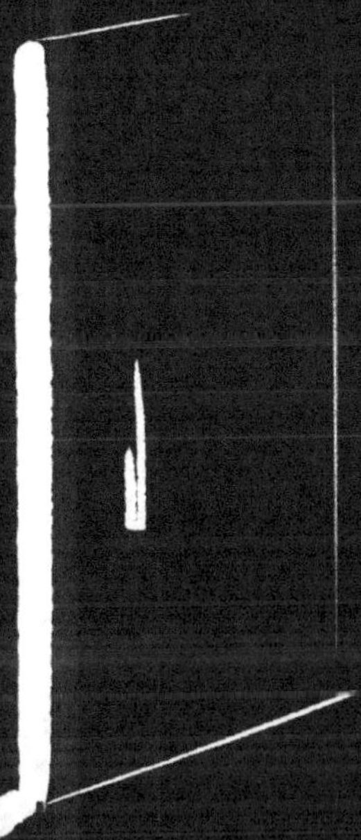

Brugge

There are beautiful cities...
and some grab the limelight,
but Brugge is serene, cute and charming

The canals lined by homes
from fairy tales,
the narrow lanes and,
the almost empty paths lifted
out of romantic novels,
the mighty cathedral facades,
the numerous swans and,
the stylish horses knocking their
hoofs hard on cobblestoned roads!

Relic

Nothing remains, but a relic of identity.
A home ravaged by knives and guns,
spattering blood, books and bangles.
The strike knows no barriers. When it hits,
it takes them all. A home, once unlocked
by its people, nourished and nurtured by
sounds, smells and songs, becomes a cave of
rubble, cracks and cobwebs. For passersby
to ignore. For onlookers to wonder. For
belongings to burn. For breathing souls to
flee. But the relic stays. It hangs, abandoned
and comatose. It stands out in irrelevance,
braving the vagaries of weather - a pale
brick red, above pools of cleaned, dried,
and now disappeared blood. The rust,
building month after month, year after year,
parallels the silent, relentless effort of the
mind to bury trauma. The thoughts of birth,
childhood, marriage, love, quarrels, and
stories, once shared by a home, live on as
flickering images, as relics of a once-thriving
identity. Homes do take birth and do die.
They are not here to stay. They do not stay
for as long as we think. To have four walls,
alive, is freedom.

An 'ekphrastic' poem is a vivid, often reflective description of a work of art.

Hymn

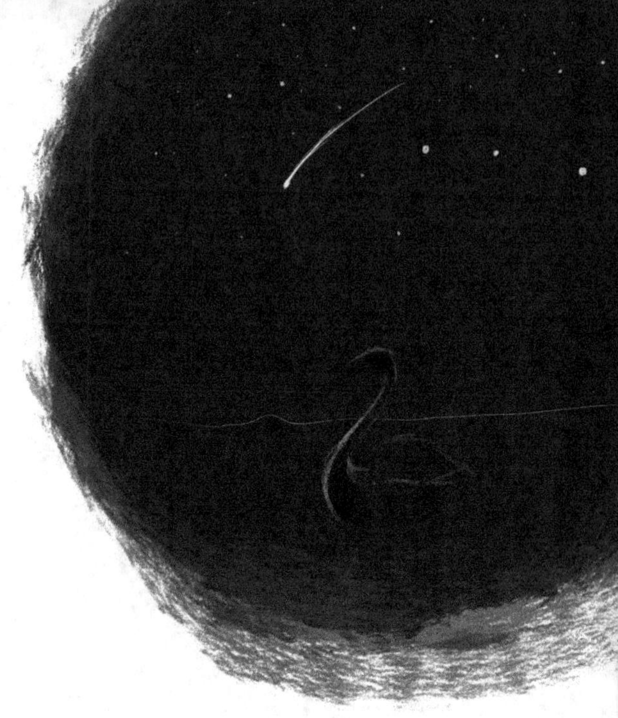

"My rhythm, a hymn
at a far dawn,
A star that falls,
as a black swan.
Shh! says my hand
that wants a catch
Naah! says a Myth
that draws a snatch"

*This is a "Lipogram" - a poem in which the only vowel
is A. Consonants are allowed, but E, I, O & U are not.*

"Your childhood hunger is the one that never leaves you."

- Chitra Banerjee Divakaruni

About the Author

Ameya Bondre's writing has been featured on several platforms such as *Mumbai Live, The Bombay Review, Café Dissensus (New York City/India), Visual Verse (London/Berlin), The Sunflower Collective, Inkspire [June 2020], Delhi Wire, Pune Mirror, the Bookish Elf, Letters to Strangers, and Oxford Bookstore (New Delhi),* and it has received a narration via *BookMyShow*. Ameya is the author of *"Afsaane"*, a collection of short stories on relationships, hope, conflict and acceptance, which received rave reviews since its release in December 2019. Ameya shuttles between Mumbai, Bhopal, and Bengaluru. He is also a trained physician (KEM Hospital, Mumbai) and a healthcare researcher with honours from Johns Hopkins University (alumnus), MIT and TEDx. Within a hectic work-life, Ameya is currently drafting a novel.

Credits

Cover Picture by Kai Cheng

Content-page Picture by Jackson Henry

Introduction page Picture by Tsunami Green

All Photographs sourced from Unsplash.com

www.ingramcontent.com/pod-product-compliance
Lightning Source LLC
Chambersburg PA
CBHW070551160726
48003CB00005B/2004